D0643778

Stink bugs
33305234115339
1en   12/23/15

Stink Bugs

by Mari Schuh

Bullfrog
Books

Ideas for Parents and Teachers

Bullfrog Books let children practice reading informational text at the earliest reading levels. Repetition, familiar words, and photo labels support early readers.

Before Reading
- Discuss the cover photo. What does it tell them?
- Look at the picture glossary together. Read and discuss the words.

Read the Book
- "Walk" through the book and look at the photos. Let the child ask questions. Point out the photo labels.
- Read the book to the child, or have him or her read independently.

After Reading
- Prompt the child to think more. Ask: Have you seen a stink bug? What was it doing? Did it smell?

Bullfrog Books are published by Jump!
5357 Penn Avenue South
Minneapolis, MN 55419
www.jumplibrary.com

Copyright © 2015 Jump! International copyright reserved in all countries. No part of this book may be reproduced in any form without written permission from the publisher.

Library of Congress Cataloging-in-Publication Data

Schuh, Mari C., 1975– author.
 Stink bugs / by Mari Schuh.
    pages cm. — (Insect world) (Bullfrog books)
 Audience: Age 5.
 Audience: K to grade 3.
 Includes bibliographical references and index.
 ISBN 978-1-62031-164-6 (hardcover: alk. paper) —
 ISBN 978-1-62496-251-6 (ebook)
 1. Stinkbugs—Juvenile literature. I. Title.
II. Series: Schuh, Mari C., 1975– Insect world.
 QL523.P5S38 2015
 595.7'54—dc23
                                              2014031369

Series Editor: Rebecca Glaser
Series Designer: Ellen Huber
Book Designer: Michelle Sonnek
Photo Researcher: Michelle Sonnek

Photo Credits: All photos by Shutterstock except:
age fotostock, 16–17, 17, 20–21, 23tl, 23br; Corbis, 8;
Dreamstime, 15; Nature Picture Library, cover;
Thinkstock, 6–7, 23bl.

Printed in the United States of America at
Corporate Graphics in North Mankato, Minnesota.

Table of Contents

Smelly Bugs

Spring is here.
A stink bug wakes up.

It looks for food.

The stink bug crawls.

It is slow.

See its wide body?

It looks like a shield.

Uh-oh. A bird is hungry.
The stink bug is
in danger.

The stink bug hides.
It looks like tree bark.

The stink bug gives off a bad smell.

Phew! It is stinky!

The bird flies away.

Now the stink bug is safe.

It sucks plant juice.
It uses its long beak.
Slurp!

beak

17

The stink bug eats bugs, too.

Winter is coming.
The stink bug finds
a warm place.

It hides under a log.

It rests until spring.

Parts of a Stink Bug

antenna
A feeler that a stink bug uses to smell and feel.

body
A stink bug's body is wide.

leg
A stink bug has six legs, like all insects.

wings
Stink bugs have thick front wings and thin back wings.

Picture Glossary

beak
The pointed part of a stink bug's mouth.

shield
A piece of armor used to protect the body; stink bugs are shaped like shields.

crawl
To move slowly.

suck
To draw into the mouth; stink bugs use their beak to suck plant juice and sap.

Index

To Learn More

Learning more is as easy as 1, 2, 3.

1) Go to www.factsurfer.com

2) Enter "stink bugs" into the search box.

3) Click the "Surf" button to see a list of websites.

With factsurfer.com, finding more information is just a click away.